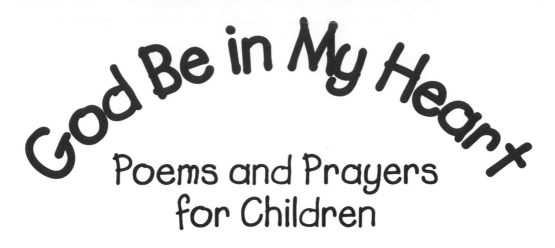

God Be in My Heart

Poems and Prayers
for Children

Written, Selected, and Illustrated

by Laurie Lazzaro Knowlton

Boyds Mills Press

POQUOSON PUBLIC LIBRARY
500 CITY HALL AVENUE
POQUOSON, VIRGINIA 23662-1996

Except where authorship is noted, the poems and prayers in this book are anonymous in source. Every effort has been made to locate all rights holders. If an oversight has occurred, we will be glad to rectify the situation in future editions.
All biblical quotes are from the New International Version of The Holy Bible.

Text and illustrations copyright © 1999 by Laurie Lazzaro Knowlton
All rights reserved

Published by Bell Books
Boyds Mills Press, Inc.
A Highlights Company
815 Church Street
Honesdale, Pennsylvania 18431
Printed in China

Publisher Cataloging-in-Publication Data

God be in my heart / compiled and illustrated by Laurie Knowlton.
—1st ed.
[32]p. : col. ill. ; cm.
Summary: A collection of short prayers and inspirational poems for young children.
ISBN 1-56397-646-3
1. Children—Prayer books and devotions—Juvenile literature.
2. Children's prayers. [1. Prayers and devotions.] I. Knowlton,
Laurie. II. Title
291.4/3'220—dc21   1999   AC   CIP
Library of Congress Catalog Card Number 98-71793

First edition, 1999
Book design by Laurie Lazzaro Knowlton.
The text of this book is set in 16-point Souvenir.
The illustrations are done in fabric collage.

10 9 8 7 6 5 4 3 2 1

To my creator
and to all those who believe in me,
with special thanks to Karen.

—L.L.K.

"My heart leaps for joy,
and I will give thanks to him in song."
—Psalm 28:7

God's bird in the morning
I'd be!
I'd set my heart
within a tree—
Close to His bed
and sing to Him
Happily—
Happily,
a sunrise hymn.

For rosy apples, juicy plums,
And honey from the bees,
We thank you, heavenly Father God,
For such good gifts as these.

The earth has got a carpet
All shining fresh and green.
It's made of little blades of grass
With flowers in between;

And on this carpet,
Gay and free,
We dance our thanks,
Dear Lord, to thee.

Dear God,
Coach me in the way
That I should always play.
Please,
Let the teams see
a picture of you in me.

—Laurie Lazzaro Knowlton

Sunday, Monday, Tuesday,
God's always at my side.
Wednesday, Thursday, Friday,
My needs are satisfied.
Saturday, Sunday, Monday,
The days they come and go.
Tuesday, Wednesday, Thursday,
God loves me head to toe!

—*Laurie Lazzaro Knowlton*

Dear God,
I didn't mean to do it.
I'm sorry as can be.
I didn't mean to do it.
Please,
will you forgive me?

—Laurie Lazzaro Knowlton

Happy Birthday!

Hip-Hooray!

Thank you Jesus for this day.

All day long I'll sing your praise.

For my gifts of love and grace.

—Laurie Lazzaro Knowlton

You turned my wailing into dancing;
...and clothed me with joy,
that my heart may sing to you
and not be silent.
Oh Lord my God, I will give you
thanks forever.

—*Psalm 30:11*

Dear Lord,
Tonight
I pray for peace with all my might
That kids across the world unite
and teach our parents not to fight.

—Laurie Lazzaro Knowlton

I hear no voice, I feel no touch
I see no glory bright;
But yet I know that God is near,
In darkness as in light.

He watches ever by my side
And hears my whispered prayer
The father for his little child
Both night and day doth care.

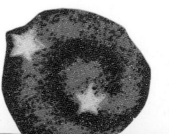

God be in my head

And in my understanding.

God be in mine eyes

And in my looking.

God be in my mouth

And in my speaking.

God be in my heart

And in my thinking.

God be at mine end

and in my departing.

—French Book of Hours, 1490

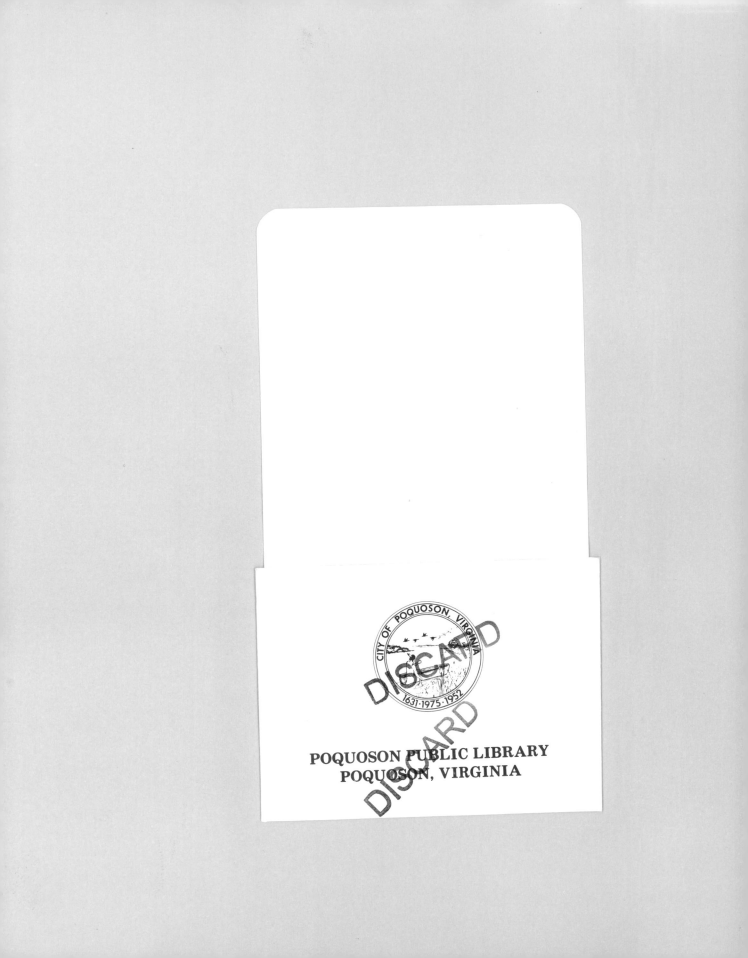

CITY OF POQUOSON, VIRGINIA
1631·1975·1952
DISCARD
DISCARD

**POQUOSON PUBLIC LIBRARY
POQUOSON, VIRGINIA**